Between The Lines

....

Sheila Kender

Copyright © 2023 by Sheila Kender

All rights reserved.

No portion of this book may be reproduced in any form without written permission from the publisher or author, except as permitted by U.S. copyright law.

Contents

1| between the tears — 1
2| between the curiosity — 6
3| between the dinner table — 11
4| between the humiliation — 19
5| between the sleeping pills — 26
6| between the promises — 29
7| between the burgers — 33
8| between the library doors — 38
9| between the ghetto walls — 44
10| between the warehouses — 51
11| between bedfelt conversations. — 59
12| between the sea — 64
13| between the night — 71
14| between the neat freaks — 77
15| between the personal question — 81

16| between the thoughts   85

17| behind the party   93

18| between the missing remote   100

19| between the lazy performers   105

1| between the tears

Morose's POV_____BETWEEN THE LINES_____

WHEN I was younger, I would dare my father to dare me to touch crawling insects, just so I could see his reaction when I actually did it.

My mom would stand by the kitchen counter and giggle at my tactics, and maybe I would include her also, or perhaps dad was the one to smother her with attention.

That was when I thought the world was all good, that there was no evil on Earth, and that I'd be okay, as long as I was with them.

But then reality struck me at the raw age of thirteen when my mother died from being in the wrong place at the wrong time, and my father became a money and power crazed man, who married a woman for the imagery, and I had to deal with her wrath.

It wasn't all bad, I got a step brother named Ben, who was already an adult in his early twenties, but he was the sweetest thing I have ever seen, even if he despised the situation as much as me.

Still, not even money, nor a loving step brother, could have prepared me for —,

"Get out of my car." Carla, the black haired trophy wive snarls and I step out, grateful to be away from her. My car was currently getting repaired due to nonsensical high school pranks, and just because we were wealthy, didn't mean we had a garage filled with cars.

Carla sped off, and I let out a loud huff as I stared at the place before me.

How I hated high school,

Even worse,

A private high school.

Filled with snobby rich teenagers, who looked at you like you were scum, simply because your skin color didn't match theirs. Or maybe you just weren't as skinny and fit.

Letting out a soft noise of agony, I walk into the halls with my head down.

I find my first class, which was English, and take plop in my usual table at the back, the teacher ignoring me since she had long given up on trying to keep me out of her class when we had an entire thirty minutes before the bell rang.

I removed my notebook, my name scrawled beautifully on the cover. Something my mom had giving me, painted and decorated herself.

I open it up, and run my hands over the first page, that she had written a short note on.

To my babygirl, Morose,May you find peace in this notebook,May you write your goals, your aspirations and everything you are going to be. I believe in you,I love you,Mummy,Rose,

A napkin appears in front of me and I frown, looking up to find a pair of concerned dark brown eyes.

My eyes drop to his outstretched hands and I take the napkin from him.

"Thank you." I murmur, dabbing my eyes gingerly.

Jenin, the school's queen rolled her eyes at me in disgust and it's then I realized that I must've been crying for the entire thirty minutes.

Wow.

"No problem." He took a seat next to me, and I sniff, tucking my book away.

Marcus White, that was the boys name.

He wasn't a bad boy, he wasn't a jock, he wasn't a nerd. He just existed. A normal boy who came to school, learned, and went on with his day.

That was how I really knew who he was. I liked how simple his life was.

There was no rumors about him beating up some freshmen in the halls, or having a string of broken hearts trailing behind him, just a plain ole' boy.

He had a skin complexion that matched mine, the color of chocolate, and a diamond stud that was kept clean on his right ear. He was tall, taller than me, which was saying something because I wasn't short. At all.

He wore the normal look of a white tee, and ripped skinny jeans with vans, signature silk waves layer beautifully on his head.

There was no debating that he was handsome.

I looked away, not wanting to make him uncomfortable.

If there's one person in the school who doesn't think I'm a freak, why ruin it?"

{ Between T H E Lines}

"Pathetic. Don't you have any friends?" Jenin mocks, as she stands over me at my lunch table.

"Jenin, can you just go away, I don't have time for this." I sigh, and she snorts.

"What? Need some space to sl—,"

"One more word, just one more and I reorganize your face." I stand quickly, squaring up to her and she easily cowers back, but puts on her front as she glares at me.

"I don't know who you think you are but—," a loud slam breaks us out of the tense moment, the entire cafeteria watching us.

Marcus sat at my table, his face black as he stared at Jenin. He had slammed his tray on the table.

What was he doing here?

"Excuse yourself, I need to speak to Morose." He says smoothly, and Jenin simply gapes, before giving off a frustrated noise and stomping away.

He knows my name.

I slowly sit back down, cautious of what was happening. I've gone through enough cruel jokes and pranks for this year alone.

"Hi." I mutter and he nods, picking up his fries to eat. "Um, not that I'm, well it's just that — why are you sitting here?"

"Well, we're friends." He says, his eyes holding pure amusement.

"We are?" I actually question, as I furrow my eyebrows.

"We are."

"Since when?"

"The moment I saw those tears hit the paper." I frown.

"You were watching me." I say, more as a statement and he shrugs.

"I was. You're a beautiful girl."

This was strange. This was really strange. It must be a prank. Yup, that's what it was. Another, careless joke, that always left me humiliated.

I gather my stuff, "okay, whatever's supposed to happen now, I don't want to deal with it. At least not today." I stand and he gives me a confused glance.

"What are yo—," But I was already out of earshot as I walked away, more unshed tears lining my eye lids.

2| between the curiosity

Morose's POV　　　　　　　　　　BETWEEN THE LINES

"Pizza or Chinese?" Ben questions as we drive home and I shrug.

"Whatever you like." He doesn't say anything, just let's put a soft sigh, as he usually does. "Have you been to your therapist?" He asks.

"Yes."

"And?"

"And?" I repeat sharply and he closes his mouth, causing me to feel guilty. "And. . . She says I'll be fine."

He puts his hand over mine and squeezes, throwing me a soft smile which I try to return.

We end up at a diner, not to far from home. "We're eating together. Let's go."

I remove my seat belt and trudge behind him slowly, his curls bouncing slightly over his forehead, his green eyes cold and calculating.

I did that.

I turned a high spirited young man, into a man who was always on edge, always protective.

He barely hung out with his friends, it was just work, then me. And although I loved the company, I was taking up his life.

But all of that would change. I wrap my arms around myself as the Air conditioning from inside hits me. Only eleven more months and he would be free.

"What are you feeling for?"

"A burger. Maybe some fries?

"Apple soda or sprite?"

"Arizona." He pouts and I can't help but giggle, choosing a booth to slide into. He waits on the side, and my feet bounces from under the table.

A habit I had when I realized I didn't have the notebook with me. The door chimes, and I frown as Marcus and an unrecognizable female walks in. He was laughing at whatever she said, and I looked away so I wouldn't appear to be eavesdropping or desperate.

A tray appeared in front of me, and it was then I realized that I was hungry.

The smell of freshly salted fries had my mouth watering, I wasted no time putting them into my mouth.

"Slow down their gorilla." Ben snorts and I roll my eyes at him. "How was school?" My eyes immediately dart to the boy who now sat across from me, he caught me staring and my eyes widen as I being the back to my food.

"It was fine." I answer tightly.

"Who is that? Is he from your school? Is he bothering you?" Ben was about to stand when I put my hands on his.

"No, no, it's fine." I murmur and he looks at me unsure. "Is everything at work okay? Did you get the investors?"

That distracted him.

Ben was a manager at some big shot business. He's been trying for weeks to get a certain investor to at least come and look over their plan.

He goes into detail and although I was nodding and shaking my head, couldn't help but be occupied by the boy who kept stealing glances at me.

- - -

"Remember, just ignore her jabs, and pretend it doesn't bother you. My mom practically feeds on fear and sadness." But I already knew that.

We enter the front of the nicely painted house, and there she sat, sipping on some white wine in her Gucci and whatever else she wasted money on.

"Ben! Oh darling, how was your day?" She stands, rushing towards him with her arms open and he forces on a smile.

"It was fine, and yours?" By this time I was making my way upstairs, ready to lock myself in when she called out to me.

"Do you mind doing something for me? The private bathroom is clogged and—,"

"Mom, she had homework and stuff to get done. I'll do it." The woman scrunches up her face, her wrinkles that she tried so hard to hide, showing without mercy.

"Ben," she stressed. "You have work, you don't have time—,"

"Sure I do. Go get your stuff done Morose, I'll take care of it." Throwing him a grateful look, I trudge up the stairs and shut my door.

My eyes skin around the room, and I remove my shoes, sitting on the bed and pulling myself up to the headboard, my knees to my chest.

This was not my room. I thought, even as this was the place I slept in each and every night.

And this was not my home. I thought, as I heard angry scoldings all the way from downstairs.

But everything would be okay. Soon.

– – –

"Have you ever read the book 'To Kill A Mockingbird'?" I jump away from my locker as Marcus starts off the conversation with the weirdest question.

"Sure," I answer timidly, pretending to be distracted and disinterested, but in all truth, I loved that book. "That's the one with Atticus, and Boo, right?"

He grins, "right. I sometimes wish I could be like Boo." I don't question him. "It's a shame really, we never really got to know what was going on in there."

"Have you ever read "The Art Of White Roses?'"

"I can't say I have." He says walking in step with me, even if I stretched my legs as far as the could reach to get away. "Tell me about it?"

"Well. . I would but, I'm going to enter my class, and it's thirty minutes earlier than you normally would. I wouldn't want to—," he enters the class, and takes a seat. Mr. Donavan looks annoyed but doesn't say anything. I sigh, taking a seat.

"I guess we're talking about Cuba then."

3| between the dinner table

M orose's POV_____BETWEEN THE LINES_____

"SO IT centers around betrayal?"

"Precisely." I reply and he frowns.

"But who betrayed who?"

"Lots of people. Adelita's father betrayed her mother with infidelity, the police and government betrays Cuba and its cities within with scandal and suspicious disappearing caused by them, the people who are supposed to protect. Actually, in my point of view, everyone in the book committed some act of betrayal, whether big or small." I murmur.

"However, there was this poem that it revolved around:

"I grow a white rose,In July as in January, For the sincere friend who Gives me his honest hand,

And for the cruel one who tears From me the heart with which I love,Thorn not whistle do I grow,I grow a white rose."

Jose Martín

By this time even the teacher had ceased what he was doing to listen to me, and before Marcus could speak up he questioned me.

"What does it all mean?" The bald headed man asked in peculiarity.

"Well, it's means to forgive. Those who have done you wrong, betrayed you, do not retaliate "thorn nor whistle do I grow," find peace within and let it go." A small smile makes it's way into my face as I an actually feel the new found excitement of explaining the book.

"Grow a white rose." I finish off, finding my own peace within, as I put them to silence.

- - -

"I never got the chance to ask you what you were referring to when you suddenly walked away yesterday." If I was lightly colored, I would've reddened with humiliation.

We sat together in the cafeteria, despite the looks thrown our way.

"I apologize for that. It's not everyday someone suddenly decides to speak to the deemed 'freak', of the school, nor call her beautiful."

"Oh." He murmurs, and I bite the inside of my cheek. "If you don't mind me asking, please don't get offended. But there was once a time we're you used to be as popular as her," he points to Jenin, who threw me a dirty look right on task.

"Then it's like you simply fell off the hierarchy chart. What happened?"

The painful memory returned, not like it ever disappeared, but it usually stayed at the back of my mind. I sigh, running a hand through my black and honey highlighted coils before giving him a small smile.

"Reality. That's what happened." If he was confused, he didn't show it as he simply nodded and we proceeded talking about harmless topics.

When you looked at Marcus from afar, he wouldn't seem like one to carry conversations the way he did.

Waiting on Ben to come get me, I noticed Marcus getting into his car, a sleek black Camaro.

His face was always unbothered, and his movements were nonchalant. His attire at first glance would have you thinking that he would use 'slangs,' and internet language in reality. Which I despised.

But he didn't.

When he smiled, it was innocent.

When he let out a chuckle, it was joyful.

When he spoke, it was to the point, and intelligently said.

He didn't offer disrespect, or roll his eyes when the teacher wasn't watching. He listened and jotted his notes, and did everything he was asked to do.

I suppose that's what had me postponing the inevitable. Or even worse, entertaining this friendship.

People who are going to die shouldn't bring more people into their lives just so they can hurt them. It's not right.

I knew that all too well. It was mostly the reason why I would keep my distance. The school wasn't all bad, and there were actually down to earth teenagers who didn't care about status, but just like everything else, I pushed them away.

So why wasn't I pushing him away?

His car stops in front of me, and I mentally scold myself. I must've looked like a freak just staring at him earlier on.

"Need a ride?"

"No, I'm alright." I smile. "Thanks though."

"No problem, y'know, I don't have your number."

Don't do it.

Don't.

"Well that's because I don't have a phone." I lie and his eyes don't widen, they just turn skeptical. Great.

I usually left my phone in my bag during school hours, so it's not like he had even seen me with it.

"You don't?" He asks, suspiciously and I shake my head. "Or you don't want to give me your number."

I hesitated.

To my surprise, he chuckles.

"Okay, how about this. Ms. Morose, can I have your email address?"

I nearly burst out laughing as the way he said it, his facial expression, and the words overall.

"You're serious?"

"Deadly," He says. "If I can't get your number then. . ."

I shake my head, pulling out a book quickly, and writing down my address.

MoroseKiner@gmail.com

"All set?" I tease as I hand it over to him, and he gives me a lopsided grin.

"All set."

A vehicle honks from behind, indicating that Marcus should probably move and I chuckle as he throws a glare at whoever was behind him.

My brother.

"Later Mo-Mo."

I scrunch up my face, ready to scold him but he simply winks and takes off. I stare at his disappearing car for a few more seconds, before turning back to my brother.

"Gorilla!" He yells happily and I groan.

"Why can't you just be quiet? Maybe greet me like a normal brother?" He pouted.

"There's no fun in that."

— — —

From: Mrs. Anderson

Prepare a presentation on The topic 'What The Education System Is Doing Wrong.'

Due in three weeks time.

•Delivered just now

Well, to sum it up, everything.

Why was I even on my gmail?

Oh I know why. Because I'm a teenage fool.

I fall back in my bed with a sigh. My pile of finished homework, sitting on my desk, and my dry phone, right on top of it.

If I played music on the speakers Ben got me, Carla would probably beat me to death with it.

Maybe that was a stretch, but she would hurt me, that's for sure.

"Morose!" Dad screams, the door slamming and I internally panic.

I'm not sure why, but there was always this terrible feeling I got whenever I was near him.

Perhaps it was the fact that he allowed Carla to hit me, because he didn't hit women, or maybe it was the fact that he would usually make me sit in his office, with 'suits' that no woman in her right mind would wear to work, simply to distract the men, and lure them into working for, or with him.

To him I was no longer his daughter, I was an item. Something that simply belonged to him, and therefore, he could do as he pleases.

Eleven more months.

As soon as I was about to open the door, it flew open on it's own.

I came face to face not with the man who brought me up, who taught me to love nor who told me to treat everyone equally, but with a simple shell.

"Why aren't you downstairs?" His skin color was lighter than mine, but it was a shade of brown.

My mother however, as beautiful as she was, could give everyone in this house a shade of her darkness and still have enough for herself.

"Pardon?" I ask confused.

"Dinner time Morose. Get downstairs."

"I'm not hungry." I murmur softly. He frowns, his eyes dropping to my chest, the my stomach, and further down.

I resisted the urge to cover up.

"Downstairs. Now." He stepped aside, and I walked in front of him quickly.

A bit irritated, I harshly threw myself next to Ben, ignoring the disapproving look from Carla.

"We have important matters to discuss." He says, upon his return and I keep my eyes on the plate, my mouth etched into a frown. Beside me, Ben sighs hopelessly, unsure of what to do. "Morose, you are to join me in a business meeting after school tomorrow."

"What does she even do at these meetings?" Ben asked, obviously agitated. I never told him, too ashamed of what he would think.

"That has nothing to do with you boy." Dad says in a warning tone.

"Well. . Morose is a seventeen year old who attends high school, she should be at home, taking care of her studies." Ben defends. And it wasn't the first time. He always opposed his parents when it came to me, even after the unfortunate happening, he always stuck up for me, when I could've never done it for myself.

"Do I need to remind you of your place in this family? You are to keep quiet as I speak to my daughter."

"She has no business being in an office filled with only perverted men looking at her like some piece of meat." If only he knew.

My father slams the table and I jump.

"Ben." Carla says in a warning tone, her eyes flickering worriedly to my father.

"You are walking on thin ice boy—," Ben abruptly stands, grabbing my hand and pulling me up with him.

He pulls me out of the front door, my father's roaring, and Carla's frantic words, meeting my ears, before the awakening of a car does.

I didn't even realize I was seated in the luxurious beast.

It was at 7 in the night, that Ben and I dressed in Pajamas, went to McDonald's and sat in silence in the parking lot.

"Would you tell me what happens when you go to the building?" He asks and my throat tighten as I resist the urge to cry. All I could offer him was a soft kiss to the forehead, as I kept my lips sealed.

It wasn't just me, but it was my nature.

It was the 'Art Of White Roses."

* * *

4| between the humiliation

Morose's POV — BETWEEN THE LINES

WHEN I first got my period, I was scared beyond my imagination.

Sheltered from the world, basically my whole life, I didn't have the privilege of learning more about our reproductive organs, and what happens.

Strangely enough, I was only eleven when it came.

My mother was the type of mother that told you that babies were delivered by birds.

I remember sitting on the bathroom toilet, sobbing until my butt went numb. She wasn't home, and my father was in the back yard getting work done. I didn't feel like I could've went to him with that situation. How awkward would that have been to tell my dad that I was bleeding from down there? What could he possibly know about it anyway? ~ My young mind's thought.

In that moment, I was confused, and I thought I was dying. Not only that, but I was afraid of dying, now I welcome death, with open arms.

"But now, I welcome death, with open," I curve my 'n' into the notebook before continuing. "arms."

"Morose." I jump. Marcus appeared in front of me, and I frown at him.

"You need to stop randomly appearing and calling my name."

"I apologize." He scratches behind his head sheepishly, a text book in his hand, resting on his thigh. "A group of friends are going over to the movies tonight, would you like to come?"

"Oh, no thanks, I don't. . . I don't do crowds. . Or groups whatever you choose to call it." He seems a little disappointed and unsatisfied by my answer.

"Well," He takes a seat next to me in class, as usual, and I close my notebook. "Why not?"

"I just don't." I answer with finality, and he eyes me. I look away timidly, and he drops whatever he had waiting on his tongue.

I pause before asking, "you didn't Gmail me last night."

Gosh that sounds so ridiculous I could almost laugh.

He smirks, "oh? Did I have you waiting by the computer?" I punch his arm playfully and he chuckles.

"I got caught up with some things at home, however, ill be sure to send you a litte Birdy."

"You know, there's this thing called the gmail app, and you don't have to—,"

"Ahh, don't ruin the moment ." He hushes, and I snort, turning away.

"Ms. Kiner, a word with you." The bald headed teacher suddenly says and I stand, offering Marcus a smile before heading over to the teacher.

"Sir?"

"I've decided that I would let you stay in this class without the throwing you a single peeved deserved look, if you read and explain the poem to the class." I frown.

"Why me? Not to be candid, but the students don't like me. Why would I put myself in the itinerary of humiliation?"

"Because I said so," He miffed, and my frown deepens. "And, you're a bright girl, with an abstruse mind, I've seen it in your past essays. Now, you'll do it tomorrow, that's all."

I don't point out that at first it was an offer, I leave it alone, and meet Marcus in the same spot, this time on his phone.

"What was that all about?" He questions as I plop back into my seat.

"Oh, nothing." I murmur.

His face contorts into one of slight irritation, and although I couldn't comprehend why, I kept quiet and allowed us our own much needed space.

— — —

Dad was picking me up.

I left class an entire five minutes early, under the pretense that I was going to the bathroom so that I could make it to the near by bus station.

I didn't want people to see me leave with him. I wasn't sure why, but it was uncomfortable.

Not a minute late he arrived, a monstrous black Range Rover humming in front of me, not the kind of vehicle you would imagine a multi-millionaire driving around on a work day.

But he wasn't normal, was he?

Normal people don't use their daughters as an item of arousal for investors.

There was no greetings as I entered, he just placed onto me a bag that smelled like A.C, most likely a new inappropriate revealing outfit.

"As soon as we arrive, put it on and come to my office."

I say nothing.

My heart felt heavy, even though I had done this many times before. I hated the men's eyes on me, like I was a piece of meat, something the wanted to handle, and practice disgusting things on.

It was mortifying.

I dreaded our arrival, and as he thought I was taking too much time to enter, he flashed his workers a dazzling smile, and subtly pushed me into the elevator.

"You know the rules, push out If you need to, sway your hips when walking in front of him, flash him flirtatious smiles when he looks at you, maybe wink, just be a seductress."

Be a whore. Was all I figured.

When we entered the top floor, I walked into the bathroom and remembered the time I tried to escape.

I didn't realize there were guards who understood what was going on,

Nor the secretaries who were instructed to call him if I was seen doing anything suspicious,

I was caught the moment my foot hit the last floor, and when I got home, I ended up with shards of glass from an alcohol bottle in my head for Clara, courtesy of my dad who stood by loving it.

Ben was on vacation.

I never tried it again, and I won't now.

Not when I only have 11 months to go, id rather not spend the first two, removing and replacing bandages.

I entered the office hoping that my eyes were no longer wet. There wasn't just one man. There were three.

My throat tightened as they all looked at me, first in shock, and after scavenging my body with their eyes, lust.

"Ah, I see you've finally made it. Men, this is my daughter, Morose. Future Heiress."

That was my cue to walk forward. The pants I had on stuck to me, more than even a second skin was, and my top was so tight that I'm sure my little rolls on my side were more than evident. The front dipped too low, my Breasts almost on full display.

I take a cautious seat next to one of the men, an indication made by my father.

"Morose, this is John, Jim, and Jack. The three owners of Audralic Industries." My eyebrows went up.

Audralic Industries wasn't one of the richest in our city. It was the richest. Affluent in many ways, there was simply no competition.

People weren't sure how they do it, but they usually shut down big time companies, companies that were successful and showed no signs of failing, were shut down in less than a day, and taken over the next.

It was a smart, and stupid choose of acquiring them as investors.

Keep your friends close, but your enemies closer the always say, and in this case, I can see it was a dangerous game for both of them, more for my father, than them.

I sat next to Jack, probably the eldest, with glowing gray hair and a chiseled jaw.

I didn't have anything to say as they stared at me, everything in me felt overwhelmed.

"Right. So, you were wondering why you should invest in me."

I zoned out the moment he began talking, it was all the same. I would force myself to day dream so that I wouldn't be able to feel their disgusting eyes on me, usually they didn't touch me, but there was a first for everything.

Jacks hands were on m thigh. I turn to look at him, as he moved them higher. Panicked, I push it away.

My father clears his throat, and I thought maybe he was going to reprimand his man, but instead he turned his harsh eyes onto me.

"Okay, we've heard you." Jim says, and I clasp my hands on my knees.

It was over.

"We agree with you, and might invest, if, we all get a moment of pleasure with your daughter."

Then, my world stopped.-

5| between the sleeping pills

Morose's POV _____ BETWEEN THE LINES _____

DAD TOLD THEM that he'd think about it.

Should I really call him dad from now on?

As soon as we got home, I brushed past a worried looking Ben and shut my door, making sure to lock it.

I crumpled before I could reach the bed and ended up simply collapsing on the floor, in a burst of sobs.

They were uncontrollable and pathetic, but the feeling of pure humiliation and disgust towards myself and everyone else was overpowering.

I just laid there, crying loudly.

This has never happened before, ever. How could he stoop so low? How could he even think of... Of—

"Morose?" Ben calls, banging on the door and I bring my knees up to my chest, muffling my sobs with the fabric of the jeans I wore to school earlier. "Morose, let me in." I sniffed.

Anything else, and I would've. But right now I wanted to peel my skin off of myself. I was to become eighteen in three months, that was too much time because my father had to give them an answer during the next two weeks, a mont for the most.

I couldn't say no, because I was property.

An unwilling sob left me again and his pounding got louder.

"Morose!" He yelled over my crying.

"What is going on here?!" Carla's voice screeches and I push my hands over my ears. I began to hyperventilate.

Ben was screaming, Carla was screaming and Dad, well I don't know where he disappeared to after he dropped me off.

My chest felt like an elephant was sitting on it, I couldn't speak, I couldn't move, I just wanted this to be over.

Why the disease chose to take so long, I don't know.

I was beginning to question it now,

Could I last these eleven months?

The sun scratched at my skin, and I let out a low groan as I sit up from the hard floor.

I felt sticky and distasteful as I stood and removed my T-shirt, stripping off my jeans.

I had no intention of going to school today. Mr. Donavan would just have to hope that 'Enotes.com' had the analysis and summary of the poem.

I walked into my bathroom, avoiding my reflection. I could already visualize my chocolate brown skin and dull brown eyes. My highlight poofy hair, flat on one side from laying on it, and the one thing that revolted me the most.

My body.

Curvy in the right places with the evidence of a semi round stomach and little rolls on the side. Maybe if I was slouched, and lack all the assets this wouldn't be happening.

I scrubbed hard at my body, my tears mixing with the ice cold water.

I just wanted to feel numb.

I step out of the shower, feeling more tired than before.

"Take the pain away." I wish upon the sleeping pill bottle, as I throw three into my mouth. I just wanted to feel so heavy, that my body would have no choice but to give into the darkness.

The darkness seemed favorable right now, the darkness seemed comforting.

I barely remember changing my clothes, much less getting into bed, but I was out like a light, the moment my head hit the pillow.

6| between the promises

Marcus's POV_____BETWEEN THE LINES_____"SHE PROBABLY did it on purpose!" Mr. Donavan ranted, as I sat in the class, only him and I.

"I don't think she did. She's not that type of person." I defend and he scoffs, turning back to his work and I sighed.

Morose didn't come to school today. Well, it could be that, or she was running late.

I hoped she was running late.

These three days have been something else. Really.

She wasn't like the loud, obnoxious girls who walked the halls like they knew it all.

Or the girls who looked at others with distaste.

She stayed in her own space, minded her own business, and barely had anything to say about anyone.

She was drama free and I loved that.

The main reason why I didn't seek to acquire any friends, was frankly because I do not think anyone at the school is trustworthy. Not even the nerds.

Some of them would remove the braces from their teeth with a screwdriver if it meant a chance of popularity.

But then, there was just everything.

She had the eyes of someone who had already given up, and I knew that type of look anywhere,

She was in trouble.

* * *

I was awakened by soft knocking on the door, my head spinning and my vision blurry.

I cleared my throat, and lifted myself trying to get accustomed to the woozy feeling as I stumbled towards the door, ready to let Ben fuss about me.

Only,

It wasn't Ben.

"Morose." I stumble back, holding my head as it began to pound.

"What. . What're you—,"

"Sit." My father says, sitting at the edge of my bed, and I wasn't one to be defiant, so I sat far away from him.

He looked at me, his eyes piercing as he seemed unsure of what to say.

"Would you like to speak first?" He offers, and I whimper, pulling my knees to my chest.

"I hate you." I whisper, and he chuckles, stretching his long trouser covered legs in front of him.

"I would too." He shrugs coldly. "Do you remember the day after your mother died?"

"No." But I did, my hear squeezed in my chest.

"You tried to run away." He starts laughing as if it was funny. "From what? I don't know. I was still the same, loving—,"

"You almost beat me to death." I say incredulously. "You acted as if you were the only one who lost her, I—,"

"So you do remember," he grins wolfishly. "The day your mother died, the old me went along with her. I just came to let you know this because I don't want you to see me as weak if I decline the offer."

I frown.

"If I do, it's only because I have better plans in store for you," he smirks. "And the best part is, you have nothing to say about it."

"I'll be eighteen in three months." I defends and I almost rejoice as his smile falters. Until it gets even wider.

"Well, we'll just have to make the most of it, won't we?"

"Get out." Another voice growls, and For the first time, Dad didn't say anything.

He knew he had won.

A tear ran down my cheek as he pats my thigh as if we were having a normal conversation then exited.

Ben slammed the door, and I stare straight forward as more tears fall.

He went onto his knees.

"What happened?" He whispered at the foot of my bed, trying to peer in my eyes. "Morose please."

"Ben." I sob, shutting my eyes as I shook my head. He stood, and wrapped his arms around me. "I can't do this." I croak.

Today, marks the first day I ever broke down in front of him, and it felt terrible.

"What can't you do? Speak to me." I just kept repeating that I couldn't go on and soon tears of his own fell too. "Morose please tell me what to do?" His shoulder shook as he held me. "Let me protect you."

I composed myself a little, trying my best to be strong for him.

"You can't. . . You can't protect me Ben. I-I, I'm sorry."

Something in him changed even more, I could feel it when he abruptly stopped crying, and when his grip tightened.

"I will always protect you."

7| between the burgers

Morose's POV_____BETWEEN THE LINES_____

"IM PRETTY SURE, the fire's out to get me, it's not like I made the choice... To let my mind stay so f—cking messy." I murmur, bobbing my head to Linkin Park and Kiiara's 'Heavy'.

I was currently in the waiting room at my doctors, and the last thing I wanted to do was be here.

The place smelled weird, and the people all looked like they were holding some sort of contagious disease.

"Ms. Kiner? Morose Kiner?"

I stared at my 'guardian,' and the old lady gave me a smile as we walked in, it was a routine.

- - -

Coffee was disgusting. With or without milk, it had a terrible taste.

Now the smell? That was a different story. As I entered the coffee shop, I plopped into a seat just to inhale the fresh beans brewing in machines.

A little after five, the place buzzed with life. Here in Syvinia, it gets cold this time a year, January - July was probably our winter.

I kept my hands clasped, my mind unable to stay on one topic. It was just running. These days have been a blur, so much of a blur, that I can barely figure out my next steps.

"Did that one day ruin all my chances? Or is your gmail app not working?"

Marcus stood above me, a small smile on his face and I let a chuckle escape my lips as he sits across from me.

"Hey."

"Hey." He repeats, staring at me and I push a lock of hair behind my ear. "Are you alright? You weren't at school for two days now."

"Oh, yea um," I clear my throat, "I just wasn't feeling well, I'm better now though." He had that "yea, right" look on his face, but he didn't say anything.

"Im glad you're feeling better." He says and I realize how pointless it was to lie to him. He saw through everything.

"Did I miss anything special?"

"Not really," he shrugs, leaning back in his seat. "Although, watch out for Mr. Donavan on Monday, he's pissed." I groan.

"That's not a wrath I want to face." I say only half joking but he laughs anyway.

"I agree."

A silence falls upon us, and I find myself more interested in my fingernails.

"So, why are you here when you obviously look like you don't even like coffee?"

"I like the smell." I admit like a complete weirdo, and to my surprise he grins.

"That's not weird at all." He flicks my noise as I narrow my eyes at his sarcasm.

"It's not." I defend.

"Well, I like the taste." He calls over the waiter. "Can I have a black coffee please, just bring a bowl of sugar." The man nods before walking off and leaving us alone again.

"Morose." He speaks up and I turn to stare at him. He had this serious expression, a questioning one. And that was never good.

"The gmail thing will obviously never work since its not as efficient and you seem to not be interested in your phone as many modern teenagers." He says in all seriousness and I clamp my jaw to keep from laughing. "So, May I, Marcus White, please have your number?"

I laughed.

I made a mistake.

And I gave it to him.

Great.

— — —

"Are you hungry?" Ben asks as I step inside, and I look around timidly.

"Where's everyone?"

"They went out. Come on." I place my keys on the table, Ben had recently picked my car up from the garage. "Ho was your day?" He questioned as he led me to the kitchen and my mouth watered as I smelt burgers.

"Uneventful." I mutter, as he placed one in front of me. He grabbed a coke from the refrigerator and I thanked him.

He looked far away.

I hated that.

I did that.

I was ruining him.

"Ben?" I whisper and his eyes snap to mine.

"Wouldn't it be nice if it was just us?"

It would.

"It would. . ." I answer, taking a bite and of course, it was heavenly.

"Then let's do it." I nearly drop the food.

"What?"

"I found a nice place that I could rent, it's a bit small, but it has two bedrooms we would make it work." I frown.

"Where is this coming from?"

"Morose, I can't- I can't see you come home broken anymore, I can't just sit by and watch as you fall further, and further into the darkness. You always held yourself together, even in the worst moments, but you broke down, I couldn't handle it. I can't get the picture of you in tears, looking so hopeless, out of my head. It's killing me Morose."

I'm killing him.

"Then you should go." I encourage.

"The both of us should." I shake my head.

"I've deprived you from such a normal life for so long B, you need to enjoy life, and - and go out with friends and hook up and get drunk—,"

"But I don't want that." He says. "I just want you to be safe."

"I can't be any more of a burden than I am now. Please go on your own."

"You are not a burden." He replies immediately. "You are my little sister, and it is my duty to protect you. You have never felt like a burden, I mean, Morose, you've held yourself up on your own even when I offered you help for so long, there was no chance for you to feel like some sort of pain. I love you, you are my only sister, and therefore I will do anything to keep you safe."

I had lost my appetite. I placed the food flat on the plate, and stared into Ben's eyes.

"Thank you, but you need—,"

"I need you to stop putting others before yourself. Morose, you're broken, and you can't find your pieces, what else are you going to do?"

What else am I going to do?

Not survive these eleven months.

8| between the library doors

Morose's POV_____B E T W E E N T H E
L I N E S_____"Don't mind the errors," ~Cr4vinz

"IT'S CRAZY ISN'T it? How Jose Martin, after being thrown in jail by he hands of his own friend, actually forgave him." I explained, my hands shaking a bit. Marcus stared at me, flashing encouraging smiles, and thumbs up here and there, while the class remained neutral.

"How many of us would've actually forgave someone, or friend for putting us in prison? I don't think any of us would. But he wrote an entire poem, white roses possibly representing surrender, but definitely representing forgiveness."

"As a little side note," I close my book filled with notes. "We should forgive people, no matter how heinous the act they did to us was. We should be able to let it out of our hearts, because if we don't," I shift my gaze to Jenin. "It will eat you alive."

_ _ _

"Have you considered being a poet?" Marcus questions as we walk towards the cafeteria, and I roll my eyes.

"You know Marcus, poets write poems, not just read them."

"So? What does that notebook you have all the time contain?" I froze.

"How do you know about it?"

"You always have it in your hand." He replies, furrowing an eyebrow. "You hide it when I arrive though."

"Oh." I resume walking and he sighs.

"Will you ever tell me what's going on?"

"What do you mean?" I play dumb as we enter the library.

"Morose, something's up. I know we've just met but I want you to feel like you can trust me." My eyes widen.

"Trust you?" It came out sharper than I intended, a short laugh leaving my lips and he takes a step back, his face etched into one of confusion.

"Yes," he nods slowly. "Trust me."

"I'm sorry." I had to end this. "I honestly don't know what I was thinking when I entertained whatever notion you had that we could be friends, but we cannot." His face doesn't change as he looks down at me, he grabs my arm and pulls me into the empty hallway. Smart choice

"You've heard about me before, I'm sure. I'm the freak who doesn't have friends, who doesn't know how to hold a conversation, I'm the freak who stays at the back of the school hoping to disappear."

Shut up.

"I'm sorry Marcus. But we can't be friends, and I can't trust you." I turn to walk away.

"Why? Because of Gray?" I froze.

"How do you know about that?" I ask immediately. My heart rate had sped up as he shook his head.

"Are you honestly shutting out everyone from your life because of some. . . Some douchebag who's in jail—?"

"Shut up." I snap. "Just. . Just shut. Up."

"You think I'll do what he did to you Morose?"

He walks towards me, and I walk backwards.

"Stop." I croak.

"You think I'll push you down the stairs? You think I'll twist your wrist? You think I'll corner—,"

"Shut up!" I scream loudly, and he winces. My chest heaves as tears fill my eyes.

"Morose. . ."

"Yes," my voice cracks. "In a collective term, I think you'll hurt me," a tear falls down my cheek as I shook my head, more at myself than him.

I turn to leave, but not before staring at him sideways and finishing my sentence.

"Because look at this, you just did."

- - -

"Kiner." I was crawled up in the library, the furthest seat away from people, yet here was Jenin, walking towards me with the fakest smile I've ever seen. "How are you?" She asks, as if she cared and I sighed.

"What is it now?"

"The deal's off." She says and my throat tightens.

"Excuse me?"

"Well, we still have a few days before the contract ends. . . But it will not be renewed."

"Why? Why are you—,"

"Because you need to go." She practically growls and I shut my eyes.

"Jenin. ."

"Look at you. Not so powerful now when you know there's nothing, and no one to protect you. I can't wait Morose, enjoy your last week of solitude." She blows me a kiss before sauntering out of the library doors.

I calmly shut the book I was reading and place my head in my hands.

Early Monday morning and I was the least excited. I was on edge, and wary.

Being a sophomore in this school, and still friendless since I moved here, was terrible. Utterly terrible.

The teenagers barely bat their eyes twice at you before going about their day, and it was then that I learnt that I was a fresh fish, and fresh fishes find their way to the way on their own.

Yet, I didn't know that there was a certain level of darkness, to even the shallowest of the sea. I didn't know that sharks could wait in areas where the could completely stay underwater.

I didn't know that fresh fishes, where a target, especially one, who was different from the rest.

Before I could comprehend what was happening, the hallways emptied out, and I was towered over by a tall shadow.

"Bang!" My head collided with my locker, and I gasp in mostly fright, collapsing.

"Why are you still here?"

Gray.

Gray was by far, the biggest danger to humanity.

He was racist, sexist and all of the wrong "ists" in the world.

He had anger problems, and you couldn't so much as breath too hard around him, or else he'd get insecure and try to beat you up.

"I—I,"

He steps on my finger and I yelp loudly. A huge rough hand slaps onto my mouth and I try to bite it off, but he only squeezes my jaw.

"Gray." I try, although it comes out muffled as he was holding my mouth. His blonde hair fell over his evil eyes as he smiles viciously.

"Morose. You are not wanted here." His hands tighten and tears spring to my eyes.

I know I wasn't wanted, but what was I to do?

"You need to leave, I don't know where, before you make me do something I'll regret." He looks at me in the eye on more time before squeezing my jaw one more time and storming off.

I sat in the corner of the hallway, rocking back and fourth as I cried.

That was only the beginning.

And me, being the fool I was, I clung onto anyone who offered a little friendship, a little hand, and I guess that's what made me think I could handle it.

These people made me believe that they had me back, but when things got bad, they left. They dumped me right back in the same hallway corner and moved on like I was nothing.

Perhaps I was nothing.

And it was going to resume, I was no longer safe.

But had I ever been?

9| between the ghetto walls

Morose's POV_____BETWEEN THE LINES_____ "Don't mind the errors," ~Cr4vinz

Ben wasn't home.

Dad wasn't home.

Carla was home.

Trouble.

"I need to speak to you." She says and I immediately frown. Her black hair was in a tight ponytail that tugged harmfully at her hairline, and her figure was covered with Gucci.

"I actually have a lot of homework to get done I—,"

"It won't take long." She presses, her hands clasped together and I sigh. I was too tired to fight. I walked towards the living room, and she cleared her throat. "Ben, is my son,"

She begins.

"And you, are Marly's daughter. I think it's best if you avoid Ben, you're not causing any good for him."

"He lives in this house? How am I to avoid him?" I ask incredulously.

"Well, I simply need you to be distant, this protectiveness he has over you will get him on the wrong side of Marley, and I do not want that." I resist the urge to roll my eyes.

"This protectiveness He has over me can't simply fade." I agrue. "It's a bond." She's up like fire, and in my face. She was taller than me, even minus the heels, but if I wanted to I could take her.

The person I couldn't, was my father, and although he claimed 'didn't hit women' , when push comes to shove, it's a different story.

I mean, just because they beat you up one and 'change' doesn't mean it's over forever.

I suppose the only real reason he changed was because he had someone to do his dirty work for him.

"Listen well little girl. You, are no good for this family. You are poison." She sneers, "and I'm sure you know, but if you are in need of reminding, you are only here because you are a somewhat valued asset to your father's company. I will not have you interfere with my son, and have him weak. He is to inherit the company and make the both of us proud while you remain a mere item, so before I am to remind you of your place, I suggest you—,"

"What is going on here?" The door shuts and I don't move my teary gaze off of Carla. She's surprised as Ben steps in but I simply step away, and crawled up the steps.

With my door shut, I collapse on my bed with a sigh. Today was the worst.

How could Marcus possibly know of Gray, of what happened. No one knew.

All they knew is that one day I was the queen of sunshine and the next I was a huge black cloud of rain.

I was the freak.

And I had no problem with them assuming it, but Marcus knowing changed everything.

What else could he have possibly known?

What else do other people know?

"Crap." I run a hand through my hair.

The look on his face wasn't vicious while he asked me a string of somewhat rhetorical questions, he looked hurt.

Did he know all along?

My journal sat at the foot at my bed but I didn't pick it up. Instead I grabbed my laptop and decided to write my essay.

I knew exactly what to write about.

\- - -

|MARCUS|

"I've been hanging around this girl." I mutter as my four friends sat on the wall. The puff of smoke from the two others barely irritating my lungs at it was merely vapor.

"A girl huh?" Martin chuckles, his fade roughly topped on his head. I roll my eyes at him, the others simply listening.

This part of town was almost abandoned, asides from a run down grocery store around the corner.

Martin, Chief, Bentley and Phor have been long time friends of mine. Despite the age difference, each of them at least five years older than me, we were the closest friends could be.

It all began when I was in a bit of trouble, I don't know how I ended up there, but I was about to get robbed, and they stepped in and didn't even ask for anything in return. They rubbed my head, and called me kid. Even now, they still do.

"Who's this lucky girl?" Phor asks, shoving his Vapor into his pocket and I shrug.

"Someone from my school." I look away and it was Bentley turn to tease.

"You got a crush now fool?" He shoved me lightly and I chuckled, sipping on the ice cold beer.

"Probably."

"What is she like?" Martin asks and I run a hand on my waves.

"She's short—,"

"Everyone's shorter than your coconut tree a—." Phor comments.

"–has these beautiful brown eyes and don't even get me started on her hair."

"Natural?" Chief finally spoke up and I grinned.

"Natural."

"Hey, what's wrong with weave? I like weave." Phor argues and I roll my eyes.

"Anyway." I clear my throat. "Everything about her is just aesthetic—,"

"Uh, don't forget buddy, not all of us are as educated as you take it easy on the big words there." Chief jokes and we all chuckle.

"Can the boy describe his obviously out of his league crush in peace?" Martin smacks Chief's head and they quiet down, staring at me.

"Well, as I was saying, she's just beautiful in a lot of ways. Her hair has these sort of golden honey highlights, and her lips are full, they kinda scream kiss me y'know?" They him in approval. "And then there's her personality, she's quiet, she stays out of peoples business—,"

"She'll survive in the hood." Phor comments.

"—she's kind too. But there's something about her... She just seems distant with the world y'know? She has this glaze over her eyes, as if everything she says is rehearsed, and it - it bothers me cause she doesn't let me in."

"How long have you known this girl?"

"Like three? Four days?"

The give me a blank look before all of them start yelling at once.

"You know nothing about girls!"

"Fool!"

"Look at him, he's an abomination!"

"Disappointment!"

"Are you really that bad with girls?" Martin rolls his eyes. "Well, what did ya expect? If something's up with her, she obviously won't tell you! She barely knows you!"

They all shout sounds of agreement and I groan.

"I suppose."

"You wanna win this girl's heart? Just get close with her, show her that you're not just with her for fun." Chief advises and I nod.

"How do you guys not have a girlfriend?" I tease and they snort.

"Because we don't wanna have none."

"Yo, can I ask a question?" Bentley says and I shrug. "Who's this girl though, can we getta' name?"

I thought, why not. It's not like they knew her.

"Morose. Morose kiner." I practically sang and as their faces fell, I wondered why.

"Bro. . . That's Ben Micco's little sister?"

"What? Is he like super protective or something?" I ask confused but the look of their face made my stomach uneasy.

"Marcus. . . Ben done found his lil sister bleeding to death in yo school's locker room." Phor says softly, which was very unlike him, but at this point my stomach was in knots.

"Not only that. But she was bout to get raped to if we didn't step in." Chief continued.

"Why were you guys there?"

"We close with Ben too, Morose's like our little sister."

I can't believe my ears.

"We fell out tho." Martin says, his eyes trained on his palm. "Morose became meat and Ben was the shell, he don't even bother calling us no more, but we understand why."

My mind was far from just sailing away as I stayed quiet, my throat burning as I tried to digest it all.

"Who did it?" Bentley shrugged.

"Some guy named Gray, he's in jail now though. Ben made sure of it. But Grays family did something to shut the whole town, or at least those who knew up, I bet them kids and your school don't even know about it." Phor shrugs.

"Guys, I think I need to go home."

"Yea kid, we get it. Just do us a favor and tell Mo we said hi, it's been a while." I nod, before shoving my hands in my pocket, and walking towards where my car was at.

I wished I had just kept my mouth shut.

10| between the warehouses

Morose's POV _____ BETWEEN THE LINES _____ "Don't mind the errors," ~Cr4vinz

FIVE THINGS THE SCHOOL DOES SUCCESSFULLY.

Now I suppose it would be the likely thing to do, beginning with the negative things,

But we should acknowledge that not everything the school does is terrible.

Top five things that my school does right.

1. Lie

2. cheat

3. encourage bullying

4. neglect the duty to educate the students of MORAL VALUES

5. neglect the topic of human rights.

Whoops! Did I say not everything the school does is terrible?

It's not my fault, as you can see, #1 is 'Lie' which everyone does very well, it's hard not to adapt to that habit.

I didn't want to go to school today.

I didn't want to look at Marcus, as he most likely tried to speak to me. I didn't want him to look at me like I was someone who was fragile, someone he had to watch his words with.

Truth is the blows to my head that Gray delivered that day did more than mess me up mentally, it caused my death, my—

"Morose,"

"I'm okay Marcus." I reply quickly walking in the direction the girls bathroom.

"Let me talk to you, I—,"

"No really, it's okay. I overreacted." I said, just to get him to leave me alone but he didn't. Instead as I was reaching for the girls bathroom he grabbed my arm and pushed me against the wall.

I felt nothing but fear as it creeped up my spine. I couldn't move. I felt paralyzed as Marcus was no longer in front of me.

Gray was.

"You're still here?" He sneers, his hands tight on my wrists and I resist the urge to cry. I try to talk but no words were leaving my mouth. Gray was back. Gray was here.

Before I knew it I was full on sobbing, skidding down the walls as Marcus reappeared in front of me.

The entire hallway had stopped what they were doing, and now stared at the freak.

"Shh," Marcus slid down with me, his hands no longer on my wrist, but gently holding my shoulders as I brought my knees up to my chest, humiliated. "There's nothing to see!" He roared at the crowd, startled, they resumed what they were doing.

"Morose—,"

"Please. Leave me alone." I croak.

"No."

"Dammit Marcus!" I snap but he doesn't flinch as I look up at him pathetically with tear stained cheeks.

"Up." He says sternly, and I huff, hoping to hide my face as he helps me off the floor. He takes my hand gently this time, and leads me outside.

He removes his keys from his pockets, and opens his Camaro passenger side for me.

"What're you doing?"

"Get in."

"Marcus—,"

"Morose just. . . Please." I look back at the school, students subtly pooling at the front of the door. I was sure to get in trouble the next day.

Screw it.

I climbed inside, and he shut the door softly before heading to his side and driving off.

"Where are we going?" I sigh as we hit a red light and he smiles.

"To visit some old friends."

"You brought me here?" My voice cracks as I stare at the familiar warehouse. "That's how you knew." I whisper, and he stays quiet, observing me.

He gets out to open my side, and hovers near the door as I simply stare at the warehouse.

"Are you coming?" He gives me one last look, before walking down the slightly green stairs.

I follow.

I knew his place all to well.

"Kid? What're you doing here? Arent you sposed' to. . Be. . At. .,"

"Some friends said Hi." Marcus crosses his arm, as I stared at the three men in front of me.

"Mo. ." Phor was the first to speak, his highlighted blue hair, more electric than ever.

Dammit, why was I crying so much today?

I don't know what to do, or even what to say as I stare at the realest people I could've called friends. The people who saved me.

"I-It's been a while." Martin stutters, as he removes himself from under the car, wiping his hands. Chief and Bentley are quiet.

They all had colors in their hair.

Chief had green, Bentley had yellow, Phor had Blue and then there was Martin with Red.

Dark skinned beauties, with hearts of gold, who simply grew up on the wrong side of town.

We ended the silence as I stepped forward and opened my arms. They practically barged into me. Phor quick to near suffocate me.

"Guys," I laugh out a sob. "You smell terrible." From the corner I hear Marcus laugh, and it was then that I had forgiven him.

He had done something that brought me a million years back, to a time where I wanted to survive.

In all but a week.

What a coincidence that he knew them huh?

Is this a sign universe?

— — —

"How's that brother of yours that never checks up on us?" Bentley asks bitterly, as we all sit in their living room.

It wasn't much, and two of them had to sit on the floor, but it was cozy.

I had a can of the iciest Diet Coke I could ever have, and some Cheetos.

"He's okay. Stressed and all. Don't feel too bad, he doesn't contact anyone, and I mean anyone." I sigh as they nod.

"And you? How are you?" Bentley asks and I chuckle softly, staring at the can in my hands.

How was I?

Destructive.

Emotional.

Frustrated.

Anxious.

"I'm hanging in there." I barely say and the room falls quiet.

"You'll be ight." Chief says, patting my shoulder, obviously unsure on how to comfort me and I nod.

"How do you guys know Marcus?" I ask, attempting to change the topic and I did as everyone erupted in laughter, everyone except Marcus.

I smirked.

"This lil boy, was about 15 when he made a wrong turn and ended up in the ghetto," Phor started off, a grin on his face.

"So, he got lost, and he done walked through these streets with an entire gold chain on his neck!" Chief yelled out in disbelief and my mouth fell open as I looked at a sheepish Marcus.

"No," I say dramatically and they all start laughing again.

"Yes," Bentley continues. "You shoulda seen his face Mo, he was practically shaking. You know em' Cayot boys?"

"Ah, okay. It makes sense. They attacked him?"

"They did. But we were near while they were, so we saved him and brought him here."

"He was a talker, but the dude was funny, so we ended up keeping him around."

"Aww." I coo at Marcus and he grunts tipping the can into his mouth.

"Be quiet." He mutter at me and I giggle, running a hand through my hair.

The four of them grinned at us, and Marcus flicked his wrist to check the time.

3:30

"I should be getting her back to school so she can get her car." Marcus stood and they nodded.

"Don't make this be the last time sis." Bentley brought me in for a hug and I embrace him.

"It won't." I sigh, as the rest of them join in.

"Well Stop standing there loser," Chief says to Marcus and he sheepishly wraps his hands around us.

This felt like home.

— — —

"You're pretty close with them." Marcus comments as we head back and a smile slips onto my face.

"Around them it's a completely new atmosphere." I admit. "You don't have to worry about who you are, or where you come from. You won't be judged by your wealth, and you're looked at as just, you. I don't have to worry about hiding myself when I'm around them. They know how to lift the mood, they know how to make you feel. . . Just. . Feel." I reply crazily.

"I understand." He says, and he flicks his tongue over his lips. My eyes drop to them, and I blink quickly before looking away. "I'm sorry about yesterday, and this morning, I—,"

"Don't worry. I know you're not like him. . And you more than just made up for it." I sigh. "Thanks Marcus."

"You're welcome." He smiles and I give him a closed lip one before we pull into the school.

It was partially empty, since the bell most likely run a good twenty minutes ago. I grabbed my bag and turned to him.

"Hey Marcus? I just. . . I'm sorry, but what I said yesterday it doesn't change now. I wish I would've said it differently, but my reasons are to protect you. We can't be friends. But I am eternally grateful for today." His face immediately changes into one of confusion before into one of nonchalance. But I could see right through it.

Just like I had thought he had hurt me,

I concluded that today, I had definitely hurt him, and I'd be lying if I said it didn't bother me.

11| between bedfelt conversations.

Marcus's POV　　　　　　　　　BETWEEN THE LINES
"Don't mind the errors," ~Cr4vinz

There was so much I wanted to say. So much I wanted to tell her.

I wanted to comfort her, to tell her that it was okay, and that I was here.

But she didn't want that.

Oof!

My glove covered hands hit the punching bag, sweat pouring down my back and face.

That bastard.

We were never close, never would I associate myself with such an egoistical prick who though he was walking on air. His attitude mended with his Sister's, Jenin, I couldn't stand them.

It's amazing how the people we usually pass by without a second glance nor thought, will have the worst stories, and will hide the most pain.

Nobody knows?

So what? He goes away and that just magically makes her feel better?

What about the silence she has to keep? Keeping it to herself, in her mind, it's toxic.

"Marcus!" My mom calls and I huff, walking away from the punching bag.

"Yea?!"

"Boy! Who do you think you're answering? I am not your little friends!" I roll my eyes and remove my gloves, trudging up the stairs.

There she stood, her hands on her hips as she scowled down at me.

"Yes mother." I tease and she narrows her eyes at me.

"Your father wanted to see you. He's in his office." She says, and I nod.

"Let me freshen up first."

"Wait." She practically skips back to the kitchen, her curly short hair falling over her eyes, shaved flat at the back. She comes back out with a tray of cookies and I grin.

"Here." I take two, placing a sweaty kiss on her cheek to which she curls her hand into a fist, and punches my arm. Her scowl now a glower.

"Ow!" I yelped, nearly dropping my cookies and she huffs, giving me a satisfied smile before disappearing. I shake my head, as I walk to my room, practically swallowing the cookies whole.

Taking a quick shower, I pull a plain white T-shirt over my head, and some knee length cotton pants.

"Dad?" I stopped by his office door, and drummed my nails on it. He looked up, a small smile gracing his face as he removed his glasses.

"Hey son, come in." I plop myself onto his office chair. My dad was in his late 50s. A bulky man, with already graying 'hair' if it could be called that.

He had brown eyes, like the rest of us, and the personality of a humble worker.

I loved him.

Ew.

"Your birthday is in a few weeks, and I was wondering if there was anything you'd like to do?"

My dad was an earlier planner, our summer vacation is already planned, and the tickets are bought.

We were in January.

"Ah not really, I'll probably just chill with my friends."

and hopefully Morose.

"Okay. If you change your mind, let me know."

"Sure thing."

|MOROSE|

Damn Marcus for letting me get so close!

It's been a week and I'm already thinking of him and ways that I have no business thinking of.

I can't believe he brought me to Chief and the crew, I can't believe he—

"Morose?"

"Hey Ben." I sigh, as I push away my laptop, my legs crossed.

He sits next to me, staring straight forward as I knew exactly what was going to happen, so I avoided it.

"I met Phor, Chief, Martin, and Bentley today." I murmur, and this immediately catches his attention.

"You did?" I nod.

"They miss you." His eyes light up, before dimming and looking forward again.

"How are they?" He merely whispers and I shrug.

"They're good. The same silly personality." I chuckle softly but Ben doesn't move an inch. I hated it. "I miss them." I whisper and he blinks, his fists were white.

"I do too." Was all he said. Nothing more. My heart broke.

I did this. I broke him to the point of... Of robot like behavior to anything that didn't involve me. He didn't deserve this.

"We should visit them sometime... They—,"

"How exactly did you get on that side of town?" His jaw was ticked and I gulped. Should I lie?

"I got a ride from a friend I—,"

"A friend that knew them? That's a coincidence." He shrugs. "I'm glad you didn't bother lying, because I drove by your school and your car was there."

"Are you skipping school Morose?" He asks and I run a hand through my hair.

"It was only today. It won't happen again."

"It should not." He confirms, finally glancing at me and I drop my eyes to my feet. He sighs. "But I'm glad you went to see them."

"Who's this friend?"

"A guy named Marcus." I reply and he immediately tenses up.

"He's not like Gray." Why was I defending him?

"I didn't say he was." Ben says simply. "Be careful please." He says, and I nod. He places a soft kiss on my forehead.

"I will."

- - -

12| between the sea

Morose's POV _____ BETWEEN THE LINES _____

Oh universe why did you do this to me?

Why did you place Marcus White into my life?

It's funny how I was the one who told him to stay away, I couldn't get him out of my mind. I couldn't get how kind he was, or how he didn't run for the hills screaming 'freak' when I crumbled.

I wish there was a way to make things simpler.

I don't want to hurt him in the end.

Tell him.

I nearly burst out laughing at the audacity of my words.

Are you out of your mind Morose? Tell him?

Ben doesn't even know, why would I even bother telling some stranger?

I bite the inside of my cheek, before grabbing my backpack and shutting my door behind me. I closed the conversation in my head abruptly and pass my dad in the hallway.

"Good morning." He greeted. My stomach churned with disgust, and I didn't bother looking at him.

"Good morning." I mumble under my breath.

"What's that?" Pain shoots up my head, as he takes hold of my hair. I squeak slightly, grabbing his hand and he drags me to stare at his sadistic smile.

"I said, good morning." I bite out and he holds me to him for another second or two, before roughly releasing me, nearly chucking me down the stairs. I run my scalp, and hide the tears as I begin to walk away.

"Jim, Jack and John will be joining us tonight, dress nicely." My heart clenched, but I didn't stop. I kept going.

I forgot about breakfast, heart hammering in my chest as I flew open my door and started the vehicle.

My tires squealed dramatically as I reversed and raced down the road.

But I couldn't run, and I couldn't hide.

— — —

I got locked in the locker room.

I sat on the floor, not exactly sure how long, my knees to my chest.

To be exact, I was locked in the boys locker room. It stunk worse than Ben's pile of socks that he refuses to wash.

There were two doors, one to the halls, and one to the court which eventually led to the fields, both were locked. No amount of screaming nor banging could help me, since the room seemed to be sound proof.

Hooray.

Not to mention this was where I was assaulted, and the only thing keeping me from pulling my hair out, was the fact that I had my notebook stuck to my chest.

Don't freak out. Breathe, breathe.

Only a few more days till February, and then it'll be ten months, don't worry Morose.

Another bell rings and I tense, hoping someone would open the door. I'm not sure who precisely pushed me in here, or why, but I have an idea that it was Jenin and her goons.

It was starting all over again. The bullying.

I closed my eyes and tried to block out the scent by breathing though my mouth. The door flies open, and I look up quickly, like a deer caught by headlights.

"Nah man, it's just— Morose?" Great. Marcus walks in with one of his friends and I blink.

"Hey. . ." I clear my throat awkwardly, standing up.

"Are you alright? What're you doing here?" He comes to stand in front of me, shirtless with only basketball shorts. Seems like P.E class had just ended which means more boys would be coming in here too. Shirtless.

I needed to get out of here.

"I'm all good. I just- I- I,"

"Let me go!"

"Shut up." Gray grunted as he carried my inside the locker room. I screamed loudly, only causing him to slam me onto the floor, delivering a quick punch swiftly. I cried this time, coughing blood as he continued to drag me in.

Before Marcus could say anything else I rushed out. His footsteps could be heard behind me as I decided to skip school all together. Ben could lecture me later, but I was out of here.

"Morose wait!"

Why couldn't he just stay away?

"Okay look," he tried his best not to grab my too roughly, as he released me as soon as he saw I turned around. "If you really want to. . To cease this friendship I won't force you to talk to me. I'll pass by you like I don't know you—,"

You don't know me.

"— I'll avoid eye contact, I'll completely leave you alone, but Morose, I need you to look me in the eye and tell me that you don't wanna be friends."

"Y-you're shirtless." I mutter, and his serious expression melts into a small smile fore a moment.

"Morose. ." He dips his head a bit so he could look into my eyes, and my heart flutters.

I open my mouth to speak but nothing comes out.

"Why? Why don't you want to be friends? I mean, it's just friends I don't see why—,"

"Marcus, I just can't okay? You're a great guy, believe me, and I—,"

"I don't care if I'm a great guy, why does it matter if I cant even get your friendship? Am I not good enough?"

"It's not that I just—,"

"Do you have a boyfriend somewhere who's controlling and doesn't want you to have any male friends?" He raises an eyebrow and I sigh.

"Marcus, I'm dy—,"

"Marcus White! Get inside and put a shirt on!" Principal Green stands, his hand on his waist as he frowns at Marcus.

Marcus sighs before looking back at me. I look away.

— — —

I'm so stupid.

No, I'm... I'm a poor fish!

Was I seriously going to tell Marcus that I was dying?

"You're crazy." I laugh awkwardly to myself as I drive to the beach. "Yup, you've lost it now."

I park in the spaces, and inhale deeply, the scent of salt and the sound of waves exciting me as I step out.

At this rate, maybe I should simply drop out.

It was empty, as everyone was either in school, or at work.

I sit close to the sea, unbuttoning my jeans for a little relief as thanked my sense of style that I wasn't wearing a black shirt in this type of sun.

The breeze made up for it though.

My life was quickly spiraling out of control.

I grabbed my pen and opened up the notebook.

My hands did something they never did before and it was then that I realized that Marcus had completely pushed things out of place in such a short time.

Dear Mom,

I have no idea why I didn't think of this sooner, writing to you, but I'm glad I thought of it now.

If you saw my life you would be so disappointed. . Especially in Dad, he's completely gone, but let's not dwell on him.

There's so much I want to tell you, but I have a little dilemma.

I met this boy.

But I'm dying mommy, I have less than a year to live and I don't want to get too involved so I can only hurt him later when I'm gone.

It's hard to push him away, because in less than three days, before I had the chance to grasp what was happening, he had already wrapped himself around my head.

What should I do?

I mean I know exactly what I should do but that's obviously not working out for me.

Should I let him in?

I almost told him that I was dying today, and it didn't feel wrong. I mean my stepbrother Ben doesn't even know.

He just texted me mom, he asked where I was.

I think I've gone crazy, because I told him, knowing that when he arrives,

Nothing will remain the same.

13| between the night

Morose's POV_____BETWEEN THE LINES_____ "Don't mind the errors," ~Cr4vinz

Footsteps sound around me and I tense as Marcus comes to sit next to me.

What have I done?

At that thought I shut off any negative feelings I had, and just allowed myself to breathe.

"Hey." He whispered and I don't know why, but I smiled.

"Hey." I whisper back and we both stare forward, looking at the sea. "You shouldn't be ditching school because of me."

He shrugs, "there's a lot of things I shouldn't be doing, I do them anyway."

Can't disagree with that.

"What are you doing out here?" He questions.

"I come here when I feel pressured." I reply, "when I need peace."

"Did I cause you to feel pressured?"

"A little. But I guess it's reasonable. If I'm just going to end our little brooding friendship it's only just that I give you a reason why, right?" I let out a little laugh and he doesn't say anything. "Truth is I can't tell you right now... However,"

I turn to look at him, and thankfully he was already looking at me.

"If you really do want to continue this friendship, I need you to be fully aware that there is a possibility that you'll get hurt." My voice cracks on 'hurt' and he furrows his eyebrows. "I won't do it on purpose, but Marcus, everything is not as it seems, and—,"

I take a deep breathe.

"And I am not what I seem."

"Is this the part where you tell me you're from another planet?" He jokes, obviously trying to cheat me up and I chuckle.

"It would be simpler if it was."

"Well, as for that, I do want to continue this friendship. If me being hurt was he problem from the beginning then you should've let me decide." He says and I run a hand through my roots. "I doubt you'll hurt me though."

I give him a sad smile, deciding to play with the sand under my legs.

Oh Marcus, you don't even know.

"Enough with this depressing stuff. I just heard that I get to continue a friendship with the coolest girl I know. This calls for a celebration."

"A celebration?"

"A celebration."

"Ceeeeeleeebration time, c'mon!" Phor yells happily as he pushes my on the swings and I roll my eyes, a wide grin on my face.

"Don't start." Bentley grumbles immediately and Phor simply ignores him, singing even louder.

Chief, Martin, Bentley and Marcus, were trying to balance on the see saw, two on each side.

Idiots.

"Mo, do you still get bullied at that white school of yours?"

"Not as much, and it's not white Phor, Marcus goes there too."

"So two little black kids and a bunch of whites. Issa white school!" Chief yells and I sigh.

"Don't be racist."

"I wasn't being racist. I was stating faxs, no printer." Chief winks and I resist the urge to cringe and facepalm.

"We can stop if you're tired Ph—,"

"Oh thank you to the heavens." He abruptly stops pushing me, causing me to lose my balance and fall on my back. "Oops."

I give him a playful glare as the others laugh it up. Night was quickly approaching, and we soon found ourself huddled on opposite sides on a park bench, with a bucket of wings and biscuits.

"When's the last time we hung out like this?" Martin nudges me and I smile softly, leaning my head into his shoulder.

"I can't remember."

"Neither can I."

"How has everything been after the. . . y'know. . Honestly?" Bentley queries, crossing his arms and I knew the jig was up.

"Honestly?" They all nod, even Marcus looked curious. "I'm barely keeping myself above water. With things at home quickly spiraling out of control, me blatanltly losing interest in school, so many things are just pulling me into the deep. I. . . I don't know how long I'll struggle before it takes me under."

They're all quiet, Bentley's jaw clenched as he stared off at no where.

"Well you have us. . . You have us who are constantly pulling at your hand to keep you above water, you have us who will be your temporary oxygen tank for when you are dragged under but you will resurface Morose. I mean look at you, I barely know you but from the little I've learned you basically have the world on your shoulders. You'll make it." Marcus stunned each and everyone of us with his words, but the four others nodded and made sounds of approval to which I could only smile to.

"Thanks guys."

"always."

We descended in silence, until a petrifying thought almost caused me to have a heart attack.

I was supposed to be at home, having dinner.

I was dead.

— —

Between having to rush everyone into their cars, and you know how that can go since the four could barely take anything seriously unless it requires aggressiveness, and having to go to school for my own car, plus bid Marcus goodnight?

The dinner was over.

There was only the usual cars in my driveway,

8:45 beeping on my dashboard.

I dreaded getting inside, so I took my time locking my car, and unlocking the front door.

"Where were you?" My father's calmly collected voice rocked pure fear in my veins.

How stupid was I not to think of an excuse? The whole time here all I was thinking about was how to evade punishment.

I was screwed.

I stayed quiet, and he stood from the kitchen stool, approaching me.

"Dad I—,"

"You humiliated me!" His cool exterior wore off as he stood in front of me. A vein popped in his forehead and I knew I was done for as he motioned for Carla to step out of the dark.

"I'm sorry." I said quickly. "I got caught up with studies at the library and—,"

Smack!

I tasted the blood before I felt the blow. My lip was busted.

Carla now stood in front of me, my dad behind her. She had a sick, satisfied smile on her face, and I couldn't help but glare at her.

"You have something to say?" She snarls.

"I told you be here for dinner and what did you do?! You disobey. I was thinking of maybe, sparing you, but no." My eyes flashed to his, and that was when the real fear settled. The look in his eyes was crazed as he grabbed my back pack from me and flung it onto the floor.

"Let's go." He says and I gape. Where was Ben?

Noticing my glance at the stairs Carla smiled. "Ben, is having a little meeting right now, he won't be back for a while."

"Where are you taking me?" I ask my father as he grabs me and shoved me out the door. He shuts it loudly behind him, and forces me into his Jeep.

My heart was racing as I thought of where we were going, and what would happen there.

Bad things were going to happen tonight, I could feel it more than ever.

14| between the neat freaks

Morose's POV_____BETWEEN THE LINES_____"Don't mind the errors," ~Cr4vinz

"Dad," I croak, eyeing his speed meter and he just ignores me. "Where are you taking me?"

We were long past our neighborhood by now, entering the richer side of town.

"You are going to apologize for making me look like a fool!" He spits and I whimper. He pulls into a gated place, where he is immediately let in. He kills he engine and practically drags me inside.

John, Jim and Jack, all stood creepily by the door as they opened it. The hair on my skin stood up as they separated allowing us to step inside.

The inside was as expected, lush and spotless. Crystal chandeliers hung from the roof and all of the decor was pure white.

"Mr. Kiner, Ms. Kiner." Jim spoke first, probably the youngest of the two in his late twenties. He had black hair, and a beard that was well kept. He was handsome, but knowing what he was capable of now changed everything. Disgusting. "To what do we owe the visit, especially in such a short time."

Dad harshly pinches me and I resist the urge to yelp.

"I-I apologize for not being there for dinner. I got- I got caught up with... With school work." Jack laughs.

"Oh Mr. Kiner, you brought her all the way here to apologize? It's okay love, there's always next time." My blood froze.

"Next time?"

"Well, Morose, your father has agreed to the deal. We'll be discussing as soon as you're ready." Jim says and I don't have a second thought as I release my dinner all over the floor.

They're welcoming behavior changes immediately.

"Disgusting." Jim snaps, moving away from me as I heave.

"Maids! Come clean this up."

"I'll take my leave now gentlemen." Dad nods, grabbing my upper hand and I groan, resisting the tears that beg to fall.

"Please. And teach her some manners will you." Jack says dryly. They stared at me like I was a germ on their skin that they could finally see.

John barely spoke, but his eyes simply glazed over with curiosity and lust.

As soon as we were outside I was slapped so hard I collapsed onto the vehicle.

"Will you please stop embarrassing me?" My father growls, stepping forward and grabbing hold of my neck.

"I-I'm sorry," I wheeze as he strangles me.

"You better be sorry, or else I will make you regret ever coming into this world." He lets me go, leaving me to rub my neck and deal with my own tears.

Too late.

― ― ―

"Hey kiddo," I was wrapped up in bed when Ben poked his head inside. It was finally Friday, and I planned to spend the remainder of my afternoon after school, drowning sleeping pills. "I didn't see you yesterday to ask you how was your day." He sits on my bed and I ignore the urge to snap, or give him a cold answer. I was in no mood for a conversation.

"It was good." I mutter and he eyes me for a moment.

"I was thinking, after school I take you out? You know, just me and you." He suggests and as much as it would be lovely to spend time with my brother, u would rather not. Not after last night.

"Oh, I actually have a lot of work to get done, I don't think—,"

"C'mom Morose. You've been working really hard nowadays. You need a break."

"I'm good Ben. I don't feel like going out today." Or ever.

"Well too bad. I just wanted to make you feel like you have a choice but you don't." He says and I groan. "Get dressed, I'm dropping you off at school."

"Please, just leave me to die." I grumble out, only half joking and he just rolls his eyes and flicks my nose before heading out.

After a shower and other normal hygienic practices. I throw on a plain white T-shirt, with blue skinny jeans and a pair of flip flops. I push my unruly hair into a band and grab my back pack and my phone.

Ben was already waiting for me outside, leaving me with Dad and Carla.

"Good morning." I murmur quickly, rushing outside to avoid any type of interaction with them.

"You ready?" Ben questions and I scoff.

"Why else would I be outside?" I answer and he frowns.

"Hey, what's up with you?" I don't answer as I climb inside his vehicle. Truth is, I didn't know how to act, nor how to behave.

After last night the last thing I wanted to do was be around people.

"Did something happen yesterday?" Ben questions as he reverses and begins our journey and I sigh.

"No. I'm just a teenager with hormones."

"Morose. . ."

"Please Ben. Not right now."

"You always say that, 'not right now,' 'not today,' when are you going to let me in? When are you going to—,"

"Never." I snap loudly, just wanting peace and his jaw clenches. "I will never let anyone in because the moment I do I will fall apart. Can't you see Ben? I'm not— I don't want to be figured out, or cured, I just want to be left alone. Okay? So please, just. . . Just leave me alone." I turn towards the window so I won't see his reaction and soon enough we're pulling into school. He stood in front of the stairs and I get out.

"Have a good day at school." He murmurs and without looking at him I mutter a thanks and shut the door.

15| between the personal question

Morose's POV_____BETWEENTHE LINES_____"Don't mind the errors," ~Cr4vinz

"The worst type of people are not the people who claim they don't understand, but the people who say they understand yet they don't. They still laugh at your situation, they don't know what it feels like y'know? Sometimes. . . Sometimes I just wish I didn't have to be here." I was inside one of the bathroom stalls, avoiding English class as I played 'Helix Jump' on my phone. Two girls stepped in, one crying and the other simply comforting.

I haven't seen Marcus for the day yet.

"Vel," The friend begins. "It gets better."

Vel let's out a bitter laugh.

"This is life Dae. It never gets better. Maybe it soothes over for a while, but comes back to hit you ten times as worse. I don't know how much longer I can take this." She whispers the last part and they're both quiet. "Anyway, let's get back to class."

They leave, and I let out a breath, running a hand over my face.

It had finally hit me that I was going to be used for my body by three men. I felt disgusted. I felt like I could already feel their hands all over me, I felt like an item.

After crying my eyes out while listening to sad music, I decided that I wasn't going to let this happen. Dad could throw all the slaps, and have Carla throw as many bottles as he liked, there was no way I was going to allow such terrible things happen to me. And if it got to the point where I couldn't do it on my own,

Then I would have to tell Ben.

– – –

"Hey."

"Hey." Marcus sits right next to me for lunch, and I eye him. He looks a bit irritated as he plops into his seat. He had a hat on backwards, and his usual skinny jeans with a red polo shirt.

"Everything okay?" I raise an eyebrow and he shrugs.

"Everything's fine." He says curtly and I nod slowly.

"Alright then, tell me, what're your plans for the weekend?"

"Nothing much, actually, I wanted to ask you," I raise an eyebrow. "Chief and the gang are hosting one of their garage parties, I was wondering if you could come?"

At the sound of Chief and the rest of the boys, I immediately felt excited, but yet, I couldn't help but feel a little hesitant at the word "party".

"Maybe." I shrug and he sighs.

"Maybe? C'mon, it would be really fun."

"No doubt." I state truthfully. I've been to these before, and they were off the charts. "But parties aren't really my scene anymore."

"Well, you have my number so you'll let me know, yea?"

"Sure."

We sit in silence for five minutes, and Marcus kept glancing at me, unsure. I could tell because his knee was practically lifting the table everything it bounced against it.

"Is there something you want to say?" I ask, slightly amused and he runs a hand over his waves.

"Well. . . I just. . . Want to ask a question?"

"What is it?" He bit his lip, and my eyes immediately follow the movement. I felt my neck heat up as I hurriedly looked away and cleared my throat softly. "Spit it out."

"How comes nobody seems to know about Gray and you?" I take in a sharp breath, the unexpected question hitting me hard as Marcus sat across from me looking more confused than ever. "I mean, everyone knew that he was a bully, but for something so big to happen and not even a peep of gossip, that's kinda weird."

I close my eyes, and hug my notebook closer to my stomach.

"I'm sorry. It must be—,"

"Come with me." I stand, reaching out my hand and he stares at it. "Come on before I change me mind." I say urgently, already aware that this was a bad idea.

But I couldn't stop myself.

You only live once and if Marcus was the only outside soul that knew what was really going on, I think I like my chances with him.

16| between the thoughts

Morose's POV_____BETWEEN THE LINES_____"Don't mind the errors," ~Cr4vinz

"A FEW WEEKS after the attack, I ended up in Gray's father's office, but Gray wasn't there because he had already been sentenced." The waves crashed against the sand peacefully and I sigh. "My dad wasn't there, but my older brother Ben was and boy, He was pissed, and didn't even want to go because he was afraid he'd kill Grays father."

Marcus sat near me, listening carefully.

"So we're all in the room and he pulls out this paper, from his desk. He says,"

"Morose, I cannot express my disappointment and sorrow for what my son has done enough, so I'm going to make you a deal." The man with the grey hair spoke. He looked anything but sorry, disappointed, yes, but not in any way pitiful.

"A deal? After all of this you want to make her a deal? Do you think that—,"

"Ben it's okay." I murmur, placing a hand on his arm.

"Right. Like I said, I am extremely sorry." The man says, his eyes moving to Ben with hidden distaste.

"You never said sorry." Ben growls out.

"Anyway, I am going to completely stop the bullying at your school. No one will hiss even a word at you, nor touch you, in exchange for your silence."

"My silence?" I raise an eyebrow.

"Yes." He nods. "No one know about the attack except for you, Ben, and the legal authorities but I've already spoken to them. I would like it keep it that way."

I let out a laugh of disbelief, my hands wringing. "Why?"

"I don't want to ruin my sons reputation—,"

"Everyone will see the offense in this file when he tries to apply for a job, for school, it doesn't make much sense." I scoff, but he just continues staring, as if he knew something and I didn't.

"He's getting his name cleared after he's released." Ben elaborates for me, his jaw ticks, and my heart drop.

"No." I saybwuicklf. "I will not allow him to live a normal life after what he did to me. He's not scarred for life, he doesn't have nightmares every night about being slammed against walls and getting his face smashed into a locker, he doesn't feel disgusted every time he sees himself, but I do. And if I have to carry this burden, it's only fair that he does too."

I turn to leave, but instead of kindly understanding, his voice turns dark instead.

"Ms. Kiner, I did want it to seem like you had a choice but you don't. Your family is almost as rich as mine, so I can't exactly affect your wealth, but I assure you, if you don't sign these papers, I will make your life a living hell."

"It's already a living hell." I almost laugh at his words, twisting the knob.

"Don't make a mistake that you won't be able to recover from, be wise Morose, think of me, and the power I have—,"

"She said no." Ben snaps.

Eventually, I had to sign it because the bullying got to a point where makeup couldn't hide a thing, and I was melanin covered so imagine that.

"That is really. . . Wow." Marcus breaths, his jaw clenched as he stared out into the Ocean.

"The contracts expiring in a few days, who knows that they'll do." I tug the ends of my hair.

"Well, what about you? What will you do?" Marcus turns to look at me.

"Nothing." I shrug.

"Nothing?"

"'Nothing."

"Morose, the contract expires and you'll be able to tell everyone! You can ruin them—,"

"Marcus, let's be smart here, the man has the ability to keep authorities hushed for years, he has money stacked up by the millions, he's well known, and well respected. People won't believe me, a mere 17 year old girl. And why after almost two years I suddenly speak up? And even if they did, he'd destroy me. So that's out of the question."

"All I heard was blah blah blah." Marcus says, and I frown. He looked dead serious as he stared at me. "Morose, you can't just. . . You can't sit back and allow people to do this to you. These people already destroyed your life, and he's just going to be prancing around in what?"

"Less than a year." I whisper as realization dawns.

"You think a restraining order is going to stop him? You think his father's words are going to stop him? I don't think so, but you, you can." I look down at my sand covered feet.

"Marcus. . ." I murmur. His hand slowly snakes around my lower back and he pulls me towards him slightly.

"We can."

Thankfully I got back to school before lunch was over, at the end of the day, I sat in my A.c filled car, following Ben's new Benz. Haha.

I hummed slightly as my fingers drummed against the steering wheel. My mind drifted to Marcus. There was a certain calm that enveloped me when I laid my head against his shoulder, and it finally settled how scared I was.

I'm just a few days who knows what terrible things they'd do. I'm not sure what excuses Jenin or her father gave them so they won't bully me, but it looks like she already gave them a heads up that they could resume soon since the jocks and cheerleaders all shared matching smirks.

But when Marcus said we, I didn't feel alone. It didn't feel like when my ex friends told me they had my back but ditched as soon as things got hot. It was like a promise.

A smile settled on my face, as with a final thought, I decided that Marcus was definitely worth breaking my most important rule for.

Ben pulls over outside of the mall and my face drops. I don't want to see more teenagers.

I get out of the car, and walk towards his. Ben was extremely tall, I thought as I walked towards him. His curls got in his eye as he leaned slightly to lock the door. He wore black fitted dress pants and a white button up. He grinned as he saw me and I narrow my eyes.

"You bring me to a mall!"

"I bring you to a mall!" He repeats happily, throwing his arm around my neck as he leads me inside.

"Ben." I whine. "Why are we here?"

"Why do people go to the mall?" Ben teases and I groan.

"Ben, I don't want anything."

"Good thing I didn't ask you then." He chuckles and I groan even louder.

"Let's get something to eat first?"

"I'm not hungry." I mutter bitterly and he just chuckles.

"Great, then we'll get right to it."

We entered the first shopping store and I immediately frown. It was Victoria's Secret.

Ben, realizing where he was, started stammering.

I roll my eyes at his immature behavior and fist his shirt, pulling him back outside the store. I lead him to the first clothing store I see that catered for both men and women.

"Okay, why are we really here?" I cross my arms to look at him and he avoids my eye.

"To shop for clothes and stuff Morose." I narrow my eyes at him and he sighs, running a hand through his curls. "I have a date." My mouth drops open quickly, before I squeal loudly.

"You have a date?!" I whisper yell, suddenly feeling really giddy. He let's out a breathy laugh before walking ahead of me. "Well, what's her name?"

"It's Eilena."

"Oo, pretty. Where did you meet her?"

"She's a waitress at one of the coffee stores a little outside of town, I met her when I went on a little errand."

"What's she—,"

"Ben?" He smirks at me before turning to the new voice.

"Eilena." My eyes widen at the female that stood before me. She was absolutely. . . . Not. . . My brothers usual type.

My brother liked pretty blondes and brunettes that were neat and had themselves together.

Eilena had bold red hair, that was obviously dyed, and her shirt was a few sizes too big. Her face was pretty, little freckles running across her cheek, and the lightest set of brown eyes.

I looked at Ben in bewilderment before turning back to her.

"Hi, I'm Morose, Ben's sister." Her eyes move onto me, and she forces a smile.

"Hi, I'm his girlfriend." My eyes brows shoot into my hairline.

"Eilena. ." Ben looked just as shocked at me. She breaks into laughter at our faces.

"I'm just kidding." She says, but I had a feeling she wasn't.

"Right." Ben chuckles, obliviously. "What are you doing here?"

"Just came to buy some stuff for the house, what a coincidence meeting you here!"

"Yea. . . What a coincidence." I murmur under my breath.

"I'll be right there Morose." Ben says turning to me and I raise my eyebrow. Was he. . . Dismissing me?

I see how it is. I give Eilena a slight wave before disappearing to the racks. I absentmindedly go through the hangers, and my eyes fall over a cute dress, with a floral pattern.

Curiously, I remove it to get a better look and I was honestly blown away. It was a maxi dress, but I knew it would fit me a bit tighter since I had curves. It had spaghetti straps and a little dip at the front. It was beautiful.

I was about to place it back when Ben spoke up.

"Buy it." He says.

"Nah, I didn't like it anyway." I shrug it off ready to leave and he grabs it from the place it was. "Ben."

"Morose. You would look great in it, I saw the way your eyes lit up when you got a better look, why don't you want to get it?"

Because I don't feel comfortable exposing my body anymore.

I don't want to put it on, look in the mirror and feel disgusted.

"I don't know." I murmur.

"Well, we're getting it."

And just like that, I realized that after al I may be going to a party.

I felt nervous, and even fearful. Why was I even considering this?

Because Marcus asked you.

At the thought of him I smile, his words today replaying in my mind and for the first time in a long time, I had a sense of calm.

17| behind the party

Morose's POV_____ BETWEEN THE LINES_____ "Don't mind the errors," ~Cr4vinz

PHEW, I'M GOING to a party.

Staring at myself through the full length mirror, every five minutes I would tell myself to just take off the dress and go back to sleep.

But there was something in me that felt like I needed this. I needed to go.

There was only about seven more minutes until Marcus came to pick me up, and my hands were sweating more than my forehead on a hot sunny day.

"Okay, okay, it's just a party. Just a party." Filled with teenagers who dislike you.

What if Jenin was coming?

That thought finally dawned on me and anxiety gnawed at my stomach.

"Hey. What's wrong?" Days like these I appreciated having a brother like Ben. Who didn't really have a girlfriend, nor friends. He was always there.

"I don't know if I can do this." I groan, plopping onto the bed. "And this isn't what normal teenagers wear to parties Ben, I mean isn't it a little too dressy?"

"You can change." He suggests. "But it's okay to be different, to set an example."

I run a hand through my flat ironed hair.

"Does dad know you're going?" He asks and I shake my head.

"Great, don't let him know."

"What? Why? He'll kill me if I dont."

"Well, you won't be coming home tonight so."

"Uh, yes I will. Most likely thirty minutes after the party begins." He chuckles.

"We're spending the night at my new apartment."

"Your new apartment?" I furrow my eyebrows.

"I spoke to you about it remember? We'll pack your stuff once we get back tomorrow, but I want you to—,"

"Ben. I said I wasn't sure if i was coming. You need your freedom."

"Morose, I am not leaving you here with these... Monsters. You think I don't know what the Audralic brothers are? And what they—,"

"How do you know about that?" I ask stunned beyond my own perception.

"Because I followed you and dad, I didn't intervene because I knew if I did you would get the blame for it."

"But Carla said you were—,"

"That's what I told her. When I realized she was trying to get me out of the house so bad for this meeting, I hung out at Mayson's house down the street for a bit until you came home, and then minutes later dads rushing down the street like a madman."

I was quiet, playing with my fingers as I averted my eyes.

"What happened?"

"I—,"

Beep beep!

"Nothing." I mutter grabbing my bag. "Nothing happened."

"Call me, I'll come get you when it's done. I'll pack you some clothes for hyou e night."

"Ben—,"

"Enjoy your night Morose." I send him a glare, before heading downstairs. I open up the door to find Marcus.

"Hey." He breathes out .

"Hi." I mutter shyly. He had in red vans, with a black plain T-shirt and light blue skinny jeans. He looked like any other teenage boy, yet my heart rate sped up immediately.

"You look beautiful." He lets out a small laugh. "Different." He tucks a strand of hair behind my ear, and I couldn't help but giggle. The door widens and I hold a breath as Ben stands in front of Marcus who straightens up.

"Hello, I'm Marcus, Moroses Friend." He stretches out his hand politely and Ben sizes him up before grabbing his hand tightly.

"Ben," I stress out. "He's the one who brought me to Chief and the rest." Ben's eyes slightly soften, and he finally shakes Marcus's hand.

"I'll pick her up when she's ready, so don't worry about a ride home."

"Oh." Is all Marcus says.

"You're responsible for her tonight, keep your eyes on her at all times—,"

"We're gonna be late Ben." I let out a nervous chuckle. "I'll call you, bye!"

I skip down the stairs holding the dress up at the sides.

"I'm sorry Marcus, you don't have to do any of that, you're not my babysitter." I sigh, and he waves it off.

"I don't mind. Considering all that happened before I understand why he's like this." I stay quiet before getting inside the vehicle.

"You look really, really beautiful Morose." Marcus says, and I clear my throat in an attempt to hide my shyness.

"Thank you."

- - -

Why?

Why, why, why?

My chest tightens as Marcus opens up my door, and stretches a hand for me to take.

I couldn't do this.

I—

"Hey," He crouches in front of me. "I'm here. And I'm gonna be with you all night, you don't need to worry." I just admit that it did cause a little of my paranoia to fade away, but I was still afraid.

I take his hand and step out, it feels surreal as all eye lay on me. I immediately felt self conscious as I realized that I wore the longest dress here.

There's nothing wrong with that Morose.

"Cmon," Marcus whispers against my ear and I shiver slightly as he leads me into the booming house. Surprisingly, sweat and alcoholic didn't fill my nose like usual, and there were very few familiar faces.

"Mo-Mo!"

"Chief!" I grin happily as Marcus pulls me over to them.

"I'm so happy you made it." Bentley says as I give each of them a little side hug.

"Does little Marcus here have control of them heart strings?" Phor teases wiggling his eyebrows and I roll my eyes, a small smile playing at my lips.

I felt more at ease as I realized that this wasn't just another stupid crazy teenage party, this was Chief's party, and he would never on his life do anything to put me in danger.

Why did I even think Jenin would be here?

The garage was lightly cleaned, but wasn't very dirty to begin with. The cars and tools served as a decoration.

"How you been?" Martin asks, crossing his arms slightly and I shrug.

"I've been okay, really. I mean look at where I am now." I chuckle and he grins.

"I'm proud of you. Is this you stepping out and living again?" My eyes land on Marcus who was already looking at me, a soft smile cradling his face.

Only if he's living with me.

"Probably." I say instead.

Soon the music drowns out all conversation and with a can of soda in my hand, I lean against the counter.

"How is it?" Marcus asks.

"It's great." I grin. It really was. There were no hormonal teenagers pushing up against my rear, nor forcing me to down drinks that were spiked. There were decent human beings, some whom I already conversed with.

"So is that an assured yes for further parties?" He gives me a cheeky smile and I throw my head back and how innocent he was trying to seem.

"I'm not so sure about that one pal."

"Awh cmon, you said it yourself this is great. We're here to protect you, you're enjoying yourself, and most importantly you're far away from the poor excuse of human beings that the world now has." I chuckle at that before taking another sip of coke.

"Well, ill think about it."

"Here's something else for you to think about." Marcus steps forward, and I raise an eyebrow, surprised at how relaxed I was. "Go out with me."

And just like that I was doused in a bucket of cold ice water as reality came crashing.

"Marcus. .,"

"Shh, I said to think about it, not reject me on spot." I can't help but laugh and he offers me a lopsided grin. "For now though, let's just forget."

"Forget?" A slow song begins to play and he stretches out his hand for the second time tonight, placing his can on the counter.

"Ms. Morose, will you care to join me for a dance." I also place my can down, an everlasting grin on my face as I slip my palm into his.

And that's how we spent the night, slow dancing and giggling about nothing and everything, it was an amazing break, and amazing get away, but I couldn't help but wonder, if that was just that calm before the storm.

18| between the missing remote

Morose's POV_____BETWEEN THE LINES_____"Don't mind the errors," ~Cr4vinz

Entry #2:

I think what the school does wrong mostly, which can actually be a general issue is that they scold young ladies for wearing what they wear, eg: bright colored bras under their shirts, or thin stringer tops on a hot day, or shorts, because it isn't 'appropriate," but I know it's because we think that it'll distract the boys.

Instead of concentrating on that, we should learn to teach our teenage boys, and future generation of men, to see, and control themselves, to respect women, no matter what they choose to wear, and to learn to concentrate on what's really important, it is unfair.

But it won't change will it?

* * *

"This, is your apartment?" I ask incredulously, nearly losing my footing as I spin. "This isn't an apartment Ben."

"I know, it's a penthouse, but I didn't want you to overeact and not come."

"How much did you spend on this?" I ask in the same incredulous term. "I'm sure you're not just renting it."

"I still have a little to pay off, mostly because I know the owner and he felt generous enough to not allow me to pay all of it, but just over a million, Nothing much."

I turn to face him, ready to pull my head out by the fistfuls.

"What? Marly's gonna cut me off anyway after he realizes I've left and taken you, and although I have a nice sum of money stacked in my back account, I'd rather spend his on the bigger things."

"Dad has an account with you?"

"No, he just gave me access to his account for "whatever I may need,' when he married mom." I nod.

"What do you think?" There was a beach outside, and that made me even more tempted to stay. Not to mention that I could see the entire of our city from here, it was beautiful.

"How many rooms?"

"Just three. I figured we'd need a guest bedroom if anything."

"If Eilena?" I wiggle my eyebrows and he rolls his eyes.

"Eilena and I didn't make it." I frown. "She was just another gold digger, believe it or not."

"Oh." It made me sad. The rare times my brother did decide to date, he was always heart broken, always let down.

"But, it did help me to realize that the only woman that I should be focusing on right now, is my sister." He grabs my shoulder and pulls me into a bone crushing hug. "How was the party?"

"It was good." I squeak, almost out of breath and he lets me go. "Marcus is really a good kid. He stayed with me the whole night, and I really didn't have a sip of alcohol."

"Mm, that's good, I'd like to spend some time with this Marcus, you could possibly invite him to spend a day with us."

I roll my eyes.

"We have more complicated stuff to talk about, like how were gonna explain this to dad and—,"

"Ya ya ya," Ben waves it off. "I left mom a note, we have the weekend to wing it out before one of them comes knocking on my door." He flicks my nose and I giggle slightly.

"Now, I'm gonna order some food, choose any room and get settled, your bag is on the couch. Tomorrow be up early we're going everything shopping!" He makes weird hand gestures and I stare at him blankly before he simply stops and rolls his eyes.

"You're just a party pooper."

I retrieve my bag from the living room, and sigh once I'm in silence. The waves crashing nearby had my heart thumping with excitement, with profound peace. How could my life completely change in just a few weeks?

It was terrifying how good things were, because I know that once there were good days, the bad days didn't lurk very far.

My room was a cool blue, literally, there was no ac remote, and it was stuck on the lowest number. Situated under my comforter, the coldness gave me no motivation to eat the pizza in front of me that Ben so graciously ordered. Netflix lit up the screen, but I couldn't focus on the overrated movie that was Birdbox.

It was when my phone lit up with an unread message that I realized what my night was missing.

WhatsApp*Marcus*

Hope everything is okay, sleep tight.

Me: Did you seriously just text me that at minutes to two in the morning?

I did, why?

Norhing, how'd you know I wasn't sleeping?

I didn't, I thought that you'd just see it in the morning if you didn't see it now.

Hmm, you're a strange one.

That I am.

My fingers hesitate before I continue say screw it and throw away my pride hesitantly.

Tonight was amazing. Thanks.

You're more than welcome sweet cheeks.

Ugh, do not call me that

Fine fine, anyway, I'm barely staying awake here, talk to you in the morning?

Sure, goodnight.

Goodnight.

I don't know why but I feel stupid. Letting out a loud aggravated growl/groan, I drop my head onto the bed and sigh.

I can't afford to catch feelings. That would be stupid of me, very stupid.

What would be even more stupid, is to think that even if things were looking up to me me now, that it would stop the disease that was currently growing around me head.

It won't.

Which is why everything in my mind, and life, is short lived. Because it won't last. It never does.

* * *

19| between the lazy performers

Morose's POV_____BETWEEN THE LINES_____"Don't mind the errors," ~Cr4vinz

"Can you move faster?" I glare at the back of Ben's head as I push the very heavy trolly through the aisle. After buying a whole leap of unnecessary stuff at the furniture store, Apple, and other electronic stores, we were finally at our last destination, the grocery stores.

"Don't you think dad will find it strange that his numbers are going down by the thousands."

"You're not aware of how wealthy he is, are you?" Ben turns suddenly, almost causing my to crash into him and the throw him another glare. "Every five minutes another ten grand is thrown into the account, he's not at work all the time for no reason, this man knows what he's doing."

Five minutes?

Yeesh.

"Do we really need all this st—,"

"Gosh, do you know how many people would've gladly just grabbed everything with no complaints." He raises an eyebrow and I roll my eyes.

"Whatever. Just hurry up my foot aches."

That definitely wasn't a lie, I've been up since twelve, it's four thirty right about now.

We finally made it to the cashiers, and out the door as we load the millions of plastic bags into the truck.

It's my turn to connect my phone, and the first song I play is Eden- Drugs.

"How do you listen to this crap?" He turns up his face and changes the song, I slap his hand away.

"How dare you!"

"It was terrible!"

"Oh, and you're long time 'blues' are just so melodic." I purse my lips and he nods.

"Harmonious."

I'm silenced by kiiara's Gold, and soon both of us are mumbling our own nonsense at the chorus.

"Roof is falling, love me love, oh oh the snow." I try my best not to scream at Ben's terrible interpretation at the chorus, so I simply let him do this thing.

When we arrive, he has people who bring up the groceries for our lazy selves.

After they're all in the room, we begin unpacking, only for the door bell to ring.

"Did you invite that boy?" Ben asks and I furrow my eyebrows, shaking my head.

"I didn't."

Ben shakes off his hand before leaving to get the door. I shrug it off and continue stuffing the fridge.

"Morose!" An angry voice calls and my heart clenches. I knew it.

"Get Out! Or I'll call the cops!" My father emerges into the kitchen, and I stand, utterly terrified as he glares at me.

"Let's go." He grabs my arm harshly and I was unsure whether I should fight back, or give in.

"You are not going anywhere with her." Ben growls, his fist landing on my father's face and I jump away, surprised by his actions.

"Ben. . ."

"You took her here without my permission," Marly sneers rubbing his chin. "And then you try to drain my bank account?"

"I'm not draining anything, I was making the both of us comfortable, I hope you like our new home."

"Morose isn't staying here, I'm her father, and you are not her legal guardian."

"Don't worry, I'll get there." Ben steps in front of me, crossing his arms. I was thankful that he was acting as a shield from my father's harsh gaze.

"Morose. You better get over here right now, you know what I'm capable of." He says, and I close my eyes.

Don't do it.

"Five," He counts.

"Four,"

"Three," my heart echos in my chest, he could ruin Ben. He could. . . He could. .

"Two," I cant make anyone's life worse.

"One."

"O—," before I could finish Ben spoke up.

"Leave. Before I call the cops." I peel over his arm, and my father slowly smirks.

"You will be blocked from using any, of my cards, and I will be back. Don't think you've escaped." He directs his last words at me before he leaves. The door slams, and I press my palm against the island to steady myself.

"Morose. . .," I shake my head at him. I didn't want to hear anything.

"You know what I'm capable of. "

My palms were sweaty, my legs weak. I felt light headed, and there was an unexplainable heat.

With a shaky breath, I dash upstairs and grab a coat, before leaving Ben sitting on a stool, his face desolate.

www.ingramcontent.com/pod-product-compliance
Lightning Source LLC
Chambersburg PA
CBHW071006080526
44587CB00015B/2369